THE STORY OF
CIVILIZATION

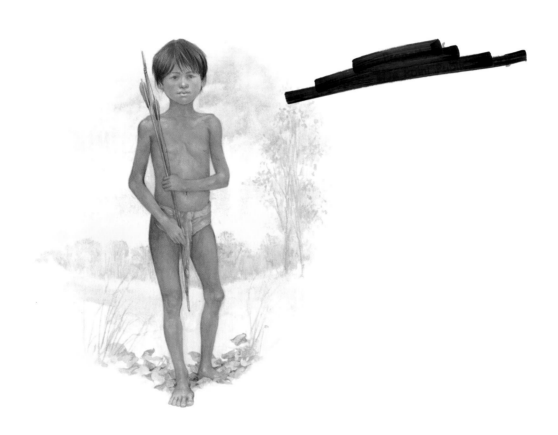

Written by

NICHOLAS HARRIS

Illustrated by

NICKI PALIN

M

The Millbrook Press

Brookfield, Connecticut

For Susan

Published in the United States in 1999 by
The Millbrook Press, Inc.
2 Old New Milford Road
Brookfield, Connecticut 06804

Created and produced by Nicholas Harris, Joanna Turner
and Claire Aston, Orpheus Books Ltd

Illustrated by Nicki Palin

Library of Congress Cataloging-in-Publication Data

Harris, Nicholas, 1956-
    The story of civilization / Nicholas Harris ; illustrated by Nicki
Palin.
        p.   cm.
    ISBN 0-7613-1257-9 (lib. bdg.)
    1. World history--Juvenile literature. 2. Civilization--Juvenile
literature. I. Palin, Nicki. II. Title.
D21.1.H345 1999
909--dc21   98-50293
                                                       CIP

Printed in Belgium

1   3   5   4   2

A long, long time ago…

People didn't live in houses or apartments.
They didn't go to stores to buy their food.
They didn't drive cars or fly in airplanes.
There were no books or televisions.
There were no cities, no towns, no villages, no farms.

People lived in the wild, along with other animals.

They learned to trap and hunt for food.
They learned to make sharp blades out of stone to use as tools.
They discovered fire—how it could be used to keep them warm, cook their food, and scare away fierce animals.

For shelter, people found caves or built tents from branches and animal skins.

Wild animals are always on the move, so people, too,
seldom stayed in one place for long.
They had to follow their food.

Hunters used wooden spears with tips made from
needle-sharp flakes of stone.
Fishermen used nets made from reeds.
The women and children gathered nuts and fruits.

Some clever people
carved bones or tusks
into the shapes of
animals or people.
Others painted
pictures or left their
handprints on cave
walls.

People discovered that the seeds of some wild grasses
could be ground up to make a powder.
This powder, flour, could be used to make bread.
They found they could plant the seeds and grow the
grasses in fields.

People had already tamed wolves—the first dogs—and
trained them to help with hunting.
Now they herded together goats and sheep and raised
them for their wool, meat, and milk.

People no longer needed to travel in search of food.
They could live and farm in the same place all year long.

They built sturdy houses using wood or clay.
They kept their seeds and grain in shelters.
They made pots to store their food.

They lived in the first villages.

People found they needed to know how to count their animals and their crops.
At first they carved pictures in slabs of clay.
Then they scratched symbols instead, each one meaning a different thing.

This was the first writing.

Some people discovered a new kind of shiny substance that they could chip out of rock.

They had discovered metal.

Over a fire it could easily be melted and made into different shapes.
Mixing different metals together made a tougher metal.
Bowls, ax heads, spear blades, knives, and other tools could be made from metal.
They were much better than wooden or stone ones.

Some people didn't work in the fields, but did other jobs instead.

Many became craftsmen, skilled at making pots, tools, or other useful objects.

Some villages grew larger and became towns, and then cities.

Each city, and the land around it, had a ruler—a king.
Some kings wanted to rule over other lands.
Battles were fought, and those who triumphed gained great empires.

People worshiped gods, praying for protection during their lives and after they died.

Kings commanded that great buildings be constructed, both for themselves and for their gods.

Not everything that people wanted could be made by
them or found nearby.
Horses might only be found a long way away.
And people from those distant lands may have had
plenty of horses, but couldn't make silk, a fine cloth.

So people got together and traded silk for horses.
Traders traveled many miles to do their business.

People swapped their goods for others at markets.
If someone wanted to trade a cow for a knife, he would
have to find someone who had a knife and who also
wanted a cow.

Such a person would be hard to find!
So people offered metal tokens, or coins, instead.
The coin was marked to show how much it was worth.
This was how money came about.

Some people spent their lives trying to find out about the world they lived in.
The first scientists wanted to know about the stars and planets and how to solve difficult mathematical problems.

Other people told stories or wrote poems.
Actors performed plays in large, outdoor theaters.

Athletes competed to see who could run or ride the fastest, jump or throw the farthest, or fight the hardest.

Engineers built all kinds of things that would improve people's lives.
They made hard-wearing paved roads.
They built aqueducts to carry water across valleys.
They constructed water mills, public baths and toilets, heating systems, and many other things.

People believed that gods created the world and somehow controlled everything that happened in it. They believed that a person had a soul, a kind of inner spirit that never died.

Different beliefs, called religions, took hold in different parts of the world.
Some people taught others the way they should live their lives.

Whole kingdoms, sometimes whole empires, would all follow one religion.

People held their beliefs so strongly they were prepared to fight for what they believed in.

Kingdoms and empires often went to war for the sake of religion.

Some empires grew rich and powerful while others
became divided up into smaller kingdoms.

People fought in wars for a lot of the time.
Kings needed the help of noblemen and warriors to lead
their armies into battle.
In return, these men were given their own lands to rule.

They became powerful, too—sometimes more powerful than the king himself.
Wars often broke out between the noblemen.

Some noblemen lived in castles, surrounded by thick walls and defended by guards, and ruled the lands all around them.

Now people lived in lands all over the world.
They lived on plains and in the mountains.
They lived in hot tropical forests, dry deserts, and on the frozen tundra.

Some lived in towns or cities.
Some lived in farming or fishing villages.
And some were content to hunt and gather fruits of the forest just as people did in the earliest days.

The houses people lived in, the languages they spoke, the food they ate, the way they worshiped, the music they played, the dances they danced, the clothes they wore—all were very different from one place to the next.

Long journeys were dangerous and hard, so people rarely traveled far.
Most people knew nothing about other places in the world.

Some people found a way to build large boats that were
sturdy enough to carry them across oceans.
Now people could travel to new lands thousands of
miles away.

Sailors set out to explore the oceans.
On their travels they discovered many new lands and
peoples they had never seen before.

Some people saw great opportunities.
They could trade with other peoples.
They could win new lands for themselves and settle
there.
They could discover gold and silver and become very
rich.

People sailed to these new lands.
In some places the people who lived there already
fought them for their land.
But the new settlers had better weapons.
They quickly took control.

All over the world, kings or emperors lived in great palaces and held great wealth and power.
They governed their lands as they wished.

But in some places people didn't want to be ruled by one all-powerful king—particularly one from a foreign land.

Some even drove out their rulers altogether.

People started to think about a fairer, better way to govern.
They would elect their leaders.
Those with the most votes would serve as the government.

But in some countries, powerful leaders took control just the same.
Countries tried to defeat others in war, just as before.

People still looked for ways to make better and stronger things.

Iron was the best metal to use.

From it people could make tools, plows, wheels, weapons, and much more.

Iron could only be separated from the rock in which it was found by heating the rock over fire.

A lot of wood was needed to fuel the fires.

Then people discovered they could use coal instead.

Large amounts of iron could now be used to make big things like bridges and ships.

Coal could also be used to heat water to make steam.
Inventors found ways of making steam engines.

Engine power was extremely useful.
It could turn wheels that could spin cloth in factories.
It could drive ships along, instead of relying on wind to
fill sails.
It could move vehicles along rails.

Many people left the countryside and came to work in
the factories in the cities.

Scientists discovered the causes of many diseases and found ways to cure them.
Now people were healthier and lived longer.
They had more and more children.
The population of the world grew.

Inventors discovered the uses of electricity, an amazing, invisible energy.
It could be used to make ovens, trains, and many other things work.
It could make lightbulbs glow for long periods.
People many miles apart could talk to each other using electrical machines called telephones.

Inventors discovered that burning oil or gas could make
engines work just as well as steam.
These new engines could be much smaller and lighter.
Now they could build a "horseless carriage."
The first cars had arrived.

From there it was only a short time before a gas engine
was added to a gliding machine, and the first airplane
took flight.

Suddenly our world became a very different place.

Cities, places of industry where people could work and earn money, grew busier and more crowded.
Roads were made smoother and cars and trucks moved faster.
People could travel by plane all over the world in just a few hours.

A very few people could travel by rocket out into space.

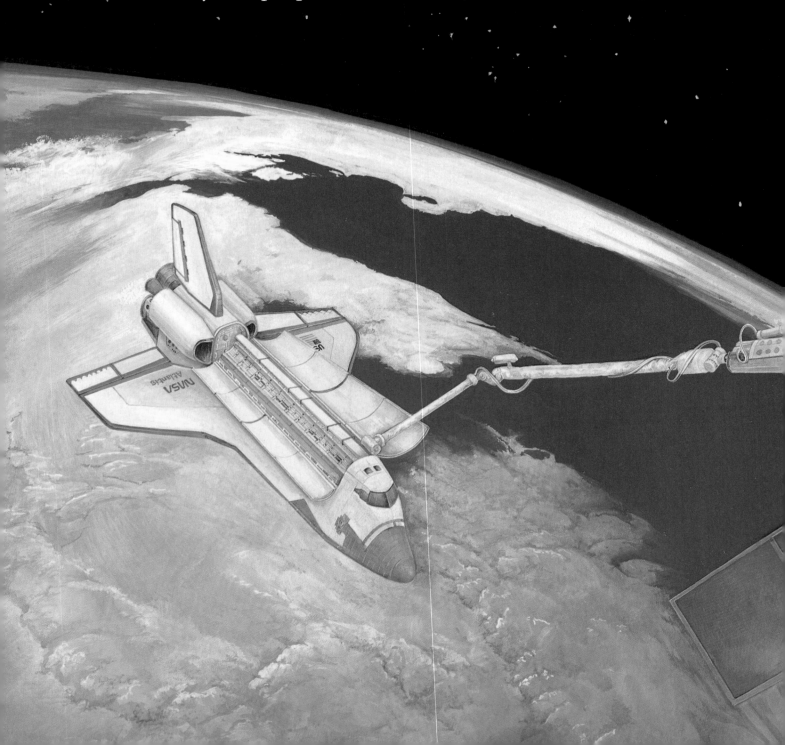

Engineers could build skyscrapers more than one hundred stories high, dam rivers to create huge lakes, and dig long tunnels under the sea.

Radios, televisions, telephones, satellites, and computers allowed people to find out about anything happening anywhere in the world in seconds.

And the population of the world kept on growing and growing.

In our world today there are rich places where people have new cars, new machines and new medicines.

There are also poor places where people cannot even feed themselves, where disease still has a deadly grip.

But when war threatens, or when we worry about the harm we may be doing to our planet, there's a very important thing to remember.
From the earliest days in the story of our world, people—working together—have used their cleverness and skillfulness to survive.

The future of our world now rests in our hands.
Let's see if we can do as well as the people before us.